The World's Worst Jokes

Edited by Victoria Fremont
Illustrations by Larry Daste

DOVER PUBLICATIONS, INC.
Mineola, New York

Bibliographical Note

The World's Worst Jokes is a new work, first published by Dover
Publications, Inc., in 2000.

International Standard Book Number: 0-486-41369-1

Manufactured in the United States of America
Dover Publications, Inc., 31 East 2nd Street, Mineola, N.Y. 11501

Note

Why are some of the best jokes the worst ones? You know the ones we mean, the kind that make you groan, roll your eyes, grit your teeth–and laugh! The jokes in this book are so bad, they're good. Some you may have heard, some not, but we think you'll find many favorites (or favorites to be) here. The pictures are a big part of the fun (you can color them too if you like).

The punch lines are upside down beneath each joke. Read them to yourself or read them aloud to friends. Have fun!

What kind of ship lies at the bottom
of the ocean and shakes?

A nervous wreck.

Why was Cinderella kicked out of
the baseball game?

Because she ran away from the ball.

Why did the lifeguard kick the elephants
out of the pool?

Because they couldn't keep their trunks up.

What did the pencil sharpener say to the pencil?

Stop going in circles and get to the point.

Why did the golfer have to change his pants?

Because he got a hole in one.

Why are fish afraid of computers?

They could get stuck in the Net.

Why did the robber take a bath before
robbing the bank?

He wanted to make a clean getaway.

Doctor, how is the boy who
swallowed the quarter?

No change yet.

Why did the ballplayer bring a
string to the game?

So he could tie the score.

What do you say to a two-headed monster?

Goodbye! Goodbye!

Why don't mountains get cold in the winter?

They wear snow caps.

Why couldn't the sailors play cards?

Because the captain was standing on the deck.

Why was the skeleton afraid to cross the road?

He didn't have the guts.

What do you get when you cross poison ivy
with a four-leaf clover?

A rash of good luck.

What is the coolest spice?

Chile.

Why was the lettuce embarrassed?

He saw the salad dressing.

How do you make antifreeze?

Hide her pajamas.

What goes all over the country but never moves?

A highway.

What do you call a snowman in April?

A puddle.

What runs but can't walk?

Your nose.

What did the teddy bear say when he was offered dessert?

No thanks, I'm stuffed.

How do you make a milk shake?

Creep up to a cow and say "Boo!"

Why did the baby strawberry cry?

Because his parents got into a jam.

If a carrot and a cabbage ran a race, who would win?

The cabbage, because it is a head.

Why did the cookie go to the hospital?

Because it felt crummy.

What is Dracula's favorite fruit?

Neck-tarines.

Why did the scientist disconnect the doorbell?

He wanted to win the NOBEL prize.

What did the astronauts think of the
restaurant on the moon?

Great food, but no atmosphere.

Why do we go to bed at night?

Because our beds won't come to us.

Why was the math book so sad?

It had too many problems.

What do you call a chicken that crosses the road, rolls in the dirt, and crosses the road again?

A dirty double crosser.

Where do baby cows eat?

At the *caf*eteria.

How do you make an elephant float?

Put it in a tub and add root beer.

What do frogs eat with their hamburgers?

French Flies.

**What did the happy volcano say to
the angry volcano?**

Don't blow your top!

What do you get if you cross a snowball
with a shark?

— Frost bite.

Why do bananas wear suntan lotion?

Because they peel.

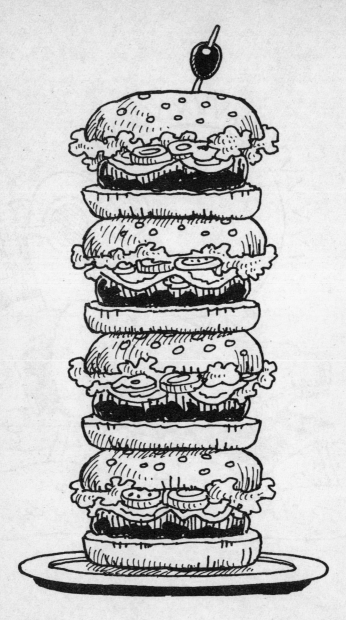

What did one plate say to the other?

Lunch is on me.

What did one tooth say to the other?

The dentist is taking me out tonight.

Why did the prune go out with the banana?

Because he couldn't get a date.

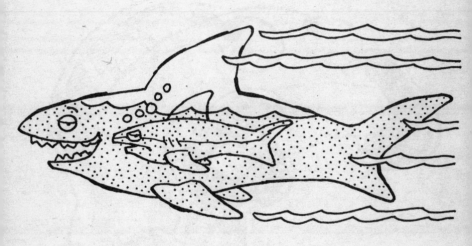

What the shark's favorite game?

Swallow the leader.

When is a car not a car?

When it turns into a driveway.

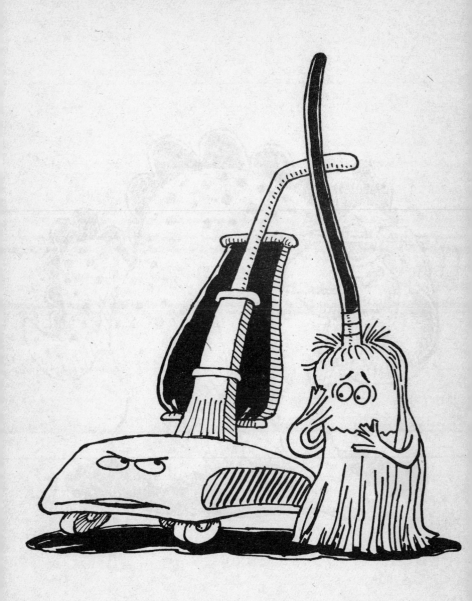

What did the vacuum say to the broom?

I wish everyone would stop pushing us around.

What do you call a blind dinosaur?

An I-don't-think-he-saur-us.

Why do opera singers make great sailors?

They're good at high C's.

Where does a sparrow go when it looses its tail?

To the retail store.

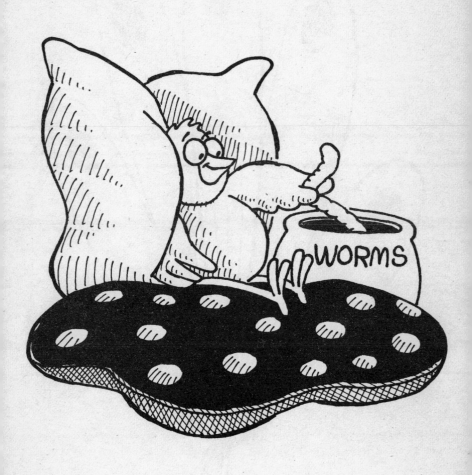

What do you give a sick bird?

Good Tweetment.

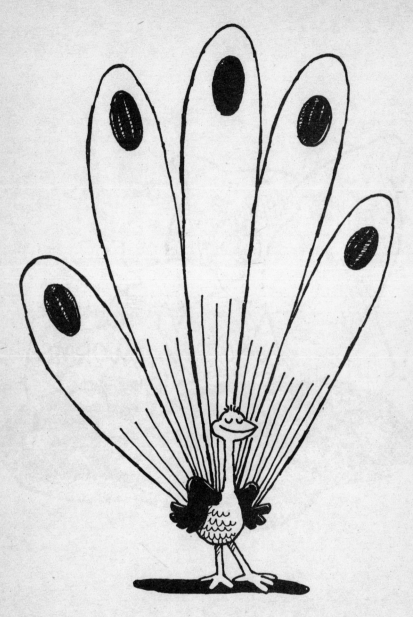

Did you hear the story about the peacock?

Yes, it's a beautiful tale.

How do chickens bake a cake?

From scratch.

Why are giraffes so slow to apologize?

It takes them a long time to swallow their pride.

Why did the skeleton go to the ball alone?

Because he had no body to go with.

Doctor, Doctor I feel like a bell!

Take these pills and give me a ring in the morning.

What is the chicken's most important
test in school?

The eggzam.

mam

What's the saddest bird?

The blue jay.

How do you make a meatloaf?

Make it go on vacation.

What fruit do ghosts like best?

Boo-berries.

What bird can lift the heaviest weight?

The crane.

**Why did the silly boy tiptoe past
the medicine cabinet?**

He didn't want to wake up the sleeping pills.

Why did the girl put lipstick on her head?

To make up her mind.

What is worse than a giraffe with a sore throat?

A centipede with sore feet.